D1159787

Guide to Rocks and Minerals

Sandstone
and Other Sedimentary Rocks

Chris and Helen Pellant

GARETH**STEVENS**

PUBLISHING

A Member of the WRC Media Family of Companies

Please visit our Web site at: **www.garethstevens.com**
For a free color catalog describing Gareth Stevens Publishing's list of high-quality
books and multimedia programs, call 1-800-542-2595 (USA) or 1-800-387-3178 (Canada).
Gareth Stevens Publishing's fax: (414) 332-3567.

Library of Congress Cataloging-in-Publication Data

Pellant, Chris.
    Sandstone and other sedimentary rocks / Chris and Helen Pellant.
        — North American ed.
        p. cm. — (Guide to rocks and minerals)
    Includes bibliographical references and index.
    ISBN-13: 978-0-8368-7909-4 (lib. bdg.)
    1. Rocks, Sedimentary—Juvenile literature. I. Pellant, Helen. II. Title.
    QE471.P356   2007
    552'.5—dc22   2006036238

This North American edition first published in 2007 by
Gareth Stevens Publishing
A Member of the WRC Media Family of Companies
330 West Olive Street, Suite 100
Milwaukee, WI 53212 USA

This U.S. edition copyright © 2007 by Gareth Stevens, Inc.
Original edition copyright © 2005 by Miles Kelly Publishing.
First published in 2005 by Miles Kelly Publishing Ltd., Bardfield Centre
Great Bardfield, Essex, U.K., CM7 4SL

Gareth Stevens editorial direction: Mark J. Sachner
Gareth Stevens editor: Alan Wachtel
Gareth Stevens art direction: Tammy West
Gareth Stevens designer: Scott M. Krall
Gareth Stevens production: Jessica Yanke

Picture credits:
All artwork courtesy of Miles Kelly Artwork Bank.
Photographs from the Miles Kelly Archives: Castrol, CMCD, CORBIS, Corel, DigitalSTOCK, digitalvision, Flat Earth,
Hemera, ILN, John Foxx, PhotoAlto, PhotoDisc, PhotoEssentials, PhotoPro, Stockbyte p. 23, p. 27; All other photographs
courtesy of Chris and Hellen Pellant.

Printed in Canada

1 2 3 4 5 6 7 8 9 10 10 09 08 07 06

COVER: **A piece of sandstone.**

Table of Contents

Words that appear in the glossary are printed in
boldface type the first time they appear in the text.

What Are Rocks and Minerals?

- Many types of rocks and minerals exist on Earth. People use them in many ways. Rocks and minerals are also beautiful to look at.

- Minerals are solid natural substances that are made of the same material all the way through. Rocks are made of minerals. They are solid, but rocks are not the same all the way through.

- One example of a mineral is quartz. If you look at a **crystal** of quartz, you'll see that it is made of the same stuff all the way through. No matter how big the piece of quartz is, it is made of the same type of material all the way through.

- Granite is a type of rock. If you look at a piece of granite, you can see that it is made of different types of minerals. Quartz, mica, and feldspar are among the minerals in granite. Limestone and marble are two other types of rock. Both contain the mineral calcite.

- Scientists who study rocks and minerals are called **geologists**.

- Geologists place different types of rocks into groups. These groups are based on how the rocks form. **Igneous rocks** form from **molten** material that cooled deep within Earth or from molten material that erupted onto Earth's surface out of volcanoes. **Sedimentary rocks** form out of layers of tiny particles. **Metamorphic rocks** form when Earth's forces heat or squeeze rocks so much that they change into a different type of rock.

- Rocks began to form about 4 billion years ago — as soon as Earth began to cool.

- The first rocks were igneous rocks. Sedimentary rocks form from rocks that have broken down. Some of these rocks are heated and squeezed until they become metamorphic rocks. If rocks are buried deeply enough in Earth's crust, they melt.

ABOVE and BELOW: Minerals can have bright colors and fine crystal shapes. The yellowish mineral ettringite (*above*) forms in six-sided crystals. Breccia (*below*) is a sedimentary rock made of large fragments of deposits that are stuck together.

What Are Sedimentary Rocks?

- Sedimentary rocks are made of **particles** that have been **eroded** or **weathered** from older rocks. For this reason, they are often called **secondary** rocks.

- The particles are carried by rivers, wind, and glaciers. While they are moving, they may become smaller, more rounded, or broken.

- Eventually, the particles are deposited. When a river slows down, for example, it can no longer carry particles above a certain weight. The particles that get left behind are called sediments.

- Over time, sediments form layers. The layers, which are also called strata or bedding, solidify into rock. Layers are the easiest feature of sedimentary rocks to see.

- Sandstone, limestone, mudstone, and shale are a few examples of well-known sedimentary rocks.

- Most sedimentary rocks form when a river flowing into the sea slows down and deposits its sediment into the sea.

- Very thick layers of sediment grow on the **continental shelves**.

- Sedimentary rocks are very important to both industry and science. In industry, for example, they are widely used to make building materials.

- Geologists look at old sedimentary rocks and compare them to newer ones. By doing this, they can figure out what Earth's environment was like in the past.

- Fossils are preserved in sedimentary rocks. Scientists learn about **evolution** by looking at fossils.

ABOVE: Sandstone is made of grains of sand compressed together or held together by minerals.

BELOW: These high sea cliffs are made of sedimentary sandstone. The strata, or layers, run horizontally.

Forming Sedimentary Rocks

- Weathering and erosion of older rocks provides the particles, or sediments, from which sedimentary rocks are made.

- Some sediments become rocks with no change to the particles. Other sediments undergo changes to their make-up as they become rocks.

- Most sediment is deposited into water. Before this sediment can become rock, the water in between the particles must be removed. Sediment can also be deposited by wind and the movement of glaciers.

- As layers of sediment are piled one on top of another, the weight of the upper layers presses the water out of the lower layers and packs the tiny pieces tightly together.

- Some sedimentary rocks are created when the weight of the layers joins grains of sand together.

LEFT: Tree roots grow into joints in many rocks. As the roots get larger, the rock is forced apart.

- Sedimentary rocks can be created when fluids that are rich in minerals seep into the spaces between particles and form a natural cement. This cement holds the particles together.

- The minerals calcite and quartz are common natural cements.

- The calcite in some sedimentary rock comes from material that was part of living creatures such as shellfish or coral.

- Many sedimentary rocks get their colors from minerals that have seeped into them as they harden.

RIGHT: In cold climates, water turns to ice in the cracks in rocks and breaks off small pieces of rock.

ABOVE: When rocks are heated and cooled in deserts, flakes of some types of rock break off to leave a rounded core.

Sandstone

- Sandstone is common sedimentary rock. It is made of sand grains compressed together or cemented by minerals.
- Sandstone can form in deserts, seabeds, rivers, and **deltas**.
- Grains of sand deposited by wind are usually round, while grains of sand deposited by water are usually angular.
- The main mineral in sandstone is quartz. Quartz is a hard, durable mineral. It can hold up to being carried a long way by wind or water before it is deposited.
- Some types of sandstone contain a lot of the mineral feldspar. Feldspar breaks down easily. When geologists see sandstone with a lot of feldspar, they think that the sediment was deposited quickly.
- Some sandstone contains **fossils**. Sandstone formed in the sea may contain fossils of **mollusks**, **brachiopods**, and **trilobites**. Delta sandstones contain plant fossils. Some of the best dinosaur fossils have been found in sandstone formed in riverbeds or on land.

LEFT: This piece of sandstone contains small, round grains of quartz that are easy to see.

- Sandstone can come in many colors. These colors are caused by the minerals in the rock. Red sandstone contains the mineral hematite. Yellow sandstone contains the mineral limonite.

- Many types of sandstone are used for building because they can easily be cut.

- Porous types of sandstone may contain water, oil, or gas. Sandstone that contains these substances can be drilled so that the substances can be removed and used.

RIGHT: The sandstone in these strata are red because they contain the mineral hematite.

Conglomerate and Breccia

- Conglomerate is a sedimentary rock made of large, rounded pebbles and rock fragments.

- The pebbles and fragments in conglomerate are usually held together with sandstone or mudstone containing quartz, calcite, or iron compounds.

- The pebbles and fragments in conglomerate can be made of many materials. Pebbles of the mineral quartz and the metamorphic rock quartzite are common in conglomerate.

- Conglomerate usually forms near the area from which its fragments come. Conglomerate is often deposited by rivers. The power of river currents is needed to move such large pieces.

- Conglomerate deposited on beaches usually contains well-rounded pebbles or cobblestones that have been rolled back and forth by waves and tides.

- Conglomerate in arid areas is the result of flash floods that move large amounts of sand and pebbles.

LEFT: Breccia is made of large, jagged fragments of sedimentary deposits stuck together.

- Breccia is a rock that is similar to conglomerate, except that it is made of jagged fragments.

- Breccia is deposited very quickly — before its fragments can become rounded.

- Many deposits of breccia form from the weathering of rock on high mountain slopes.

- When parts of Earth's crust move against one another at **faults**, a lot of rock is broken. Fault breccia is the jumble of rock fragments along the line of a fault.

ABOVE: These layers of conglomerate were formed on a river flood plain. Water carried and deposited these masses of pebbles more than 200 million years ago.

Limestone

- Limestone is a sedimentary rock that contains a large amount of the mineral calcite. A lot of calcite comes from the remains of living creatures such as coral and certain types of algae.

- Some limestone is light-colored. It can be gray, cream, brownish, or yellowish. Limestone can also be very dark in color because it contains a lot of mud or other sediment.

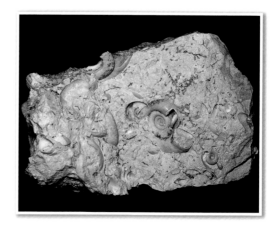

ABOVE: Limestone is often packed with fossils. The fossils seen here are the remains of water snails.

- Most limestone contains fossils. The rock may be a mass of fossils cemented together by calcite. Some types of limestone are named after the type of fossils they contain. One example is coral limestone.

- Most deposits of limestone are young compared to many types of rocks. The creatures whose remains make up limestone did not evolve until after many other types of rock formed.

- Dolostone is a type of limestone in which much of the calcite has changed into the mineral dolomite.
- Oolitic limestone is made of small, rounded grains of sediment, such as shell fragments or grains of sand. The tiny pieces develop layers of calcite around them that make them look like tiny pearls.
- Reef limestone is made from fossilized sediment **reefs**. This type of limestone can contain fossils of corals, trilobites, brachiopods, mollusks, and **crinoids**.
- Limestone is **quarried**, and it has many important uses. It is powdered for use in farming. Blocks of limestone are used in building. It is also used to make cement.

LEFT: Some limestone landscapes have a lot of bare rock.

Chalk

- Chalk is a special type of limestone. It is almost pure white and very fine grained. It is over 90 percent calcite.

- Chalk is a sedimentary rock that was deposited in the sea. It was probably deposited far from the continental shelf, in an area where there was little disturbance to the seabed.

- Almost all the calcite in chalk is the remains of living organisms. These living organisms include microscopic creatures called coccoliths.

- Chalk has almost no sand or mud in it. One reason for its purity is that the remains of living organisms that make up chalk are all that is left to be deposited in the places far from land where it forms.

- Large fossils found in chalk include ammonites and other mollusks, brachiopods, and sea urchins.

- Most chalk is found in western Europe and North America.

LEFT: Chalk is a white powdery rock made mostly of the remains of tiny sea creatures.

- Europe's chalk was deposited between 65 and 142 million years ago.
- The famous white cliffs of the southern coast of England are made of chalk.
- In the United States, chalk is found in Kansas.

BELOW: Along the south coast of England there are many high chalk cliffs. This one is called Bat's Head.

Flint

- Flint is a hard rock that occurs in small, round lumps.

- Dark bands of flint can be seen in chalk cliffs. They run parallel to the white layers of chalk.

- Flint is made of the same stuff as the mineral quartz —silicon dioxide. In spite of this, quartz and flint form in different shapes. Most quartz forms in six-sided crystals. Flint's crystals are so small that you need a strong microscope to see them.

- Flint is so hard it cannot be scratched with a a knife blade.

- Flint breaks easily into curved shapes with very sharp edges.

- The hardness and sharpness of flint makes it good for making tools.

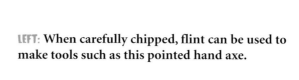

LEFT: When carefully chipped, flint can be used to make tools such as this pointed hand axe.

- Early humans used flint to make hand axes at least 2 million years ago. They made their axes by using another stone to chip pieces off of a lump of flint.
- People used flint to make tools until the early 1800s. At that time, the flintlock — a type of firearm — was still being made.

RIGHT: Lumps of flint are often dark-colored.

Ironstone

- At least 90 percent of the iron mined and quarried each year is in the form of the sedimentary rock ironstone.

- Ironstone forms in shallow water in the sea that is close to land.

- Ironstone contains minerals that contain the element iron.

- Some minerals that contain iron dissolve in water. Water carries these minerals to where sedimentary rocks are formed.

- Sedimentary rocks that contain iron are red or yellowish-brown in color.

- Many ironstones are made of small, round grains coated with minerals that contain iron.

- Very old rocks that contain a lot of iron are found around Lake Superior in the United States. They are also found in Labrador, in Canada, as well as in Ukraine, Western Australian, and Brazil.

- Iron is one of the most widely used metals. It is used in making steel, which is used in making buildings, cars, and many other things.

- The ironstone used in industry in the 19th century was only about 30 percent iron.

ABOVE: Banded ironstone is one of the richest ores of iron. This piece of banded ironstone comes from Western Australia.

Manganese Nodules

- Manganese nodules are lumps of sedimentary rock found on the floors of the Atlantic and Pacific Oceans that contain the metal manganese.

- Scientists on the research ship *Challenger* discovered them in the 1870s.

- Up to 35 percent of these lumps of rock is manganese, and each of them is about the size and shape of a potato.

- Manganese nodules develop around a grain of sediment or a small piece of a fossil. They are built in layers, like an onion. Geologists have discovered that it takes 40 million years for a 4 inch (10 centimeter) manganese nodule to develop.

- Manganese nodules are also found in the Carribean Sea and the southern part of the Indian Ocean.

- Mining the ocean floor for manganese nodules is difficult and expensive. It also harms the ocean environment.

LEFT: **This maganese nodule was taken from 16,405 feet (5,000 meters) deep in the Pacific Ocean near the Marquesas Islands.**

Stalactites and Stalagmites

- The roofs of many limestone caves are covered with hanging, icicle-like growths called stalactites. These caves also have growths rising up from the floor called stalagmites.

- Stalactites and stalagmites form when water from Earth's surface seeps down into a limestone cave.

- As water drips into the cave and **evaporates**, it leaves deposits of calcite. These deposits become slender, sometimes long stalactites.

- Stalagmites form under stalactites. Water that drips from stalactites lands on the cave floor, where it also leaves deposits of calcite. Stalagmites are usually shorter and stubbier than stalactites. Sometimes a stalactite and stalagmite grow together into a column.

- If you cut open a stalactite or stalagmite, you can see its many layers of calcite deposits.

BELOW: Stalactites grow where water that contains calcite seeps from the surface into a cave.

Deep-Sea Sediments

- In the deepest parts of oceans, strange sedimentary deposits form.

- A lot of sediment settles on the continental shelves. Very fine mud and clay are carried farther out to sea than larger particles. Slowly, this sediment settles on the ocean floor. Geologists call this sediment "ooze."

- Some deep-sea sediments are dragged into the ocean by icebergs.

- Dust shot out of volcanoes can also settle deep in the ocean.

- Some deep-sea sediments come from the skeletons of tiny sea creatures, which are made of calcite.

- An underwater landslide can drag sand and mud into the ocean. As an underwater landslide loses strength, it deposits alternating layers of sand and mud deep in the ocean.

BELOW: These sloping strata show the fine and coarse layers of deep-sea ocean sediments deposited by an underwater landslide.

Strata

- Many sedimentary rocks are deposited in neat layers that geologists call strata or bedding.

- One of the most important ideas in geology is that the strata at the bottom are the oldest and the strata at the top are the youngest.

- Fossils may be found in strata.

- Sometimes scientists find the same types of fossils in mudstone in Greenland, shale in Argentina, and limestone in Italy. When this happens, they think the strata are the same age.

- Layers of sedimentary rocks were originally deposited horizontally. When Earth's crust moves, however, the layers can be tilted or folded.

ABOVE: **When rocks are highly compressed, tight folds can be formed.**

FASCINATING FACT
If sediment is deposited without any breaks, there will be no strata. Geologists say that sedimentary rocks with no strata are "massive."

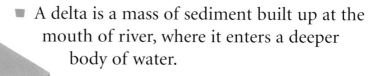

Deltas

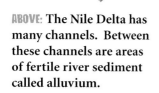

ABOVE: The Nile Delta has many channels. Between these channels are areas of fertile river sediment called alluvium.

- A delta is a mass of sediment built up at the mouth of river, where it enters a deeper body of water.

- Sediment is deposited when a river enters deeper water because the speed and power of the river suddenly decrease. With this decrease in power, the river can no longer carry the sediment, and it falls to the bottom of the water.

- The types of sedimentary rock found in deltas include mudstone and sandstone.

- Many major oilfields are in delta rocks. These include oilfields in the southern United States and Nigeria.

LEFT: This sandstone formed in a delta over 270 million years ago.

Desert Rocks

- Deserts are very dry regions that receive very little rain.

- Sandstone is one of the main desert rocks. Its grains are rounded by the wind.

- Studying the sediments of today's deserts helps geologists figure out which rocks were formed in ancient deserts.

- The strata formed by the wind are not horizontal. Instead, curved "cross-bedded" layers are formed.

- Larger fragments of quartz in desert rocks are often pitted and frosted from being blasted with sand. Mica is not usually found in desert rocks because the wind blows away its small flakes.

BELOW: Rocks formed in arid areas are often red or orange. In Arches National Park, in Utah, strata have been weathered and eroded into pillars and cliffs.

Aquifers

ABOVE: The limestone strata in these cliffs have gaps that allow water to run into them and be held underground. When there is excess rainfall, the underground water level rises and springs form along a layer of rock near the foot of the cliffs.

- An aquifer is an underground layer of rock, sand, or gravel that contains water.
- Sedimentary rocks such as sandstone, limestone, and chalk can make up big parts of aquifers.
- These sedimentary rocks can hold water because they have spaces between their grains.
- To get water out of aquifers, people drill into the layers. Water in aquifers usually has to be pumped to the surface.
- Aquifers made of sedimentary rock exist all over the United States. The Ogalla aquifer, also called the High Plains aquifer, runs through the central part of the the country. It is the largest aquifer in North America.

Uses of Sedimentary Rocks

- Sandstone and limestone are sedimentary rocks that are cut into blocks and used for building. Bricks made from mudstone are also used for building.

- Limestone and mudstone are used in making cement.

- Some sedimentary rocks trap oil under Earth's surface. By drilling into these rocks, people can pump the oil out and use it for fuel.

- Scientists use sedimentary rocks to learn about Earth's past. The many fossils that are found in sedimentary rocks such as limestone tell them about extinct creatures from trilobites to dinosaurs. The strata of sedimentary rocks tell them about changes in Earth's environment that happened long ago.

- Chalk has been used for writing on blackboards. Athletes such as gymnasts and weightlifters have also put chalk on their hands to improve their grips. Most "chalk" used today for these purposes is synthetic, or manmade.

RIGHT: **Rounded pieces of flint make up the body of this house. The framework and supports of the house are made of brick.**

Glossary

brachiopods: water animals that have a shell, no backbone, and tentacles used to push food into the mouth

continental shelves: the shallow sea areas that surround some of the continents

crinoids: sea animals with cup-shaped bodies and five or more feathery arms

crystal: a piece of a transparent mineral that can have a shape with a regular arrangement of flat surfaces and angles or a rounded shape

deltas: areas of land formed by deposits of sand and mud at river mouths

eroded: worn away bit by bit

evaporates: changes from a liquid to a gas

evolution: the slow, gradual changes that types of living beings undergo from earlier generations to later generations

faults: breaks in Earth's crust

fossils: remains of earlier types of plants and animals that are embedded in rock

geologists: scientists who study the layers of Earth and the rocks and minerals that make up Earth's crust

igneous rocks: rocks that formed from the cooling and hardening of magma

molten: melted

metamorphic rocks: rocks that have been formed by the forces of heat and pressure within Earth

mollusks: members of a group of animals, including clams and snails, that have soft bodies, no backbone, and, usually, a hard shell

particles: tiny pieces

quarried: removed from a place where rock is dug out of an open pit

reefs: ridges of rock, sand, or coral that rise near the surface of bodies of water

secondary: second in rank or importance

sedimentary rocks: rocks that formed from the small pieces of matter deposited by water, wind, or glaciers

trilobites: extinct sea creatures with segmented bodies

weathered: worn down as an effect of wind, rain, and changes in temperature

More Information

Books

Experiments with Rocks and Minerals. True Books: Science Experiments (series). Salvatore Tocci (Children's Press)

Rock Cycles: Formation, Properties, and Erosion. Earth's Processes (series). Rebecca Harman (Heinemann)

Rocks and Minerals. Science Fair Projects (series). Kelly Milner Halls (Heinemann)

Rocks and Minerals. Science Files (series). Steve Parker (Gareth Stevens)

Rocks and Minerals. Discovery Channel School Science (series). Anna Prokos (Gareth Stevens)

Web Sites

The Dynamic Earth: Plate Tectonics and Volcanoes
www.mnh.si.edu/earth/text/4_0_0.html
From the Smithsonian Institution, this Web site features multimedia presentations on how Earth's plates move and how volcanoes work.

The Dynamic Earth: Rocks and Mining
www.mnh.si.edu/earth/text/3_0_0.html
Also from the Smithsonian Institution, this Web site features great pictures.

Rock Hounds
www.fi.edu/fellows/payton/rocks/index2.html
Information about how rocks are formed and how to collect rocks, along with quizzes and puzzles.

Publisher's note to educators and parents: Our editors have carefully reviewed these Web sites to ensure that they are suitable for children. Many Web sites change frequently, however, and we cannot guarantee that a site's future contents will continue to meet our high standards of quality and educational value. Be advised that children should be closely supervised whenever they access the Internet.

Index

DATE DUE
